The Little
Duck Hunter

The Little Duck Hunter

Labrador Puppies and the Promise of Things to Come

Text and Photography by Lee Thomas Kjos

Ducks Unlimited, Inc.
Memphis, Tennessee

Author/Photographer: Lee Thomas Kjos
Book Design: Doug Barnes

Published by Ducks Unlimited, Inc.
John A. Tomke, President
Julius Wall, Chairman of the Board
D. A. (Don) Young, Executive Vice President

ISBN: 1-932052-01-1
Published September 2002
Ducks Unlimited, Inc.
Printed in Canada

Library of Congress Cataloging-in-Publication Data

Kjos, Lee Thomas. The little duck hunter :
Labrador puppies and the promise of things to
come / text and photography by Lee Thomas Kjos.
p. cm.
ISBN 1-932052-01-1 (hardcover : alk. paper)
1. Labrador retriever--Juvenile literature. I. Title.
SF429.L3 K573 2002
636.752'7'0222--dc21
2002012670

Ducks Unlimited, Inc.

Ducks Unlimited conserves, restores, and manages wetlands and associated habitats for North America's waterfowl. These habitats also benefit other wildlife and people. Since its founding in 1937, DU has raised more than $1.6 billion, which has contributed to the conservation of over 10 million acres of prime wildlife habitat in all 50 states, each of the Canadian provinces, and in key areas of Mexico. In the U.S. alone, DU has helped to conserve over 2 million acres of waterfowl habitat. Some 900 species of wildlife live and flourish on DU projects, including many threatened and endangered species.

Call to Action

The success of Ducks Unlimited hinges upon each member's personal involvement in the conservation of North America's wetlands and waterfowl. You can help Ducks Unlimited meet its conservation goals by volunteering your time, energy, and resources; by participating in our conservation programs; and by encouraging others to do the same. To learn more about how you can make a difference for the ducks, call 1-800-45-DUCKS.

Dedication

To my girl, for seeing something in me when I was young that the others did not.

Acknowledgments

In 1994, the greatest waterfowler of them all died. I sorely miss my conversations with the old man; his sage advice has stood the test of time.

That old waterfowler once asked me one day how work was going, and I replied, somewhat apathetically, "good." Wrong answer! His hackles raised, he barked back, "Not that work, your life's work!"

I was much too young at the time for such wisdom, but those words had some teeth in them. It has been some years now since the old duck hunter left the blind, but I have a hunch he would be happy to know that the little duck hunter is now doing his life's work. Thanks, Dad.

No work, no matter the depth of the project, can be completed alone. That said, I would like to give thanks to those who have made my life's work more rewarding.

Mom, for your unwavering love and patience. Thanks for taking the time to haul me around to all those sloughs when I'm sure you had something you would have rather been doing.

Diane, Cheryl, and Tom. You always made me feel special.

Karmen, Luke, and Gretchen. I can't imagine my life without you guys.

Doc. It's a rare time when you cross paths with someone who helps you blaze a new trail. I see more trails in the future.

To my partners, Bruce, Jon, Gar, Steve, Ron. You know who you are and, more importantly, what you mean to me. Thanks for putting up with such nonsense as my trying to take pictures at the most inopportune times...like when the light is just right and I flare all the birds.

To the puppies, and all of the little duck hunters that came before them.

And to the ducks. Without them, I wouldn't be doing any of this.

Anyway, I hope you enjoy the book.

Contents

Introduction

ike little magic beans, puppies are the seeds from which grow the loyalty and love of a dog. Living with dogs, having raised them up from puppyhood, is a journey no one can ever come away from without being forever changed. You can't help but see the world differently after bringing up a pup. Especially little Labrador retrievers, those little duck hunters we adore.

Our affinity for Labrador retrievers is evident by their popularity. To find a Labrador retriever (and somebody who loves Labs), you don't have to look very far. Just go find a waterfowl hunter. Two out of three share their blind with a black, yellow, or chocolate Lab.

Labs are natural-born water dogs, built for swimming and frosty morning vigils waiting in the blind on the duck marsh. Consider their webbed paws and strong front legs, barrel chest, high rear hips, and thick, otter-like tail. Even those that weren't bred for hunting share these traits (if they didn't, they wouldn't be Labs), and therefore might surprise you with what they know.

You don't have to hunt to get carried away by the power of a Lab. But if you have a Labrador retriever and you've never seen him hunt, you're missing out on what could be an amazing experience.

There's an old saying that children are for people who can't have dogs. It's one of those funny expressions that turn the original idea—in this case, that dogs are for people who can't have children—on its head. But Labrador retriever owners, especially, recognize an element of truth in it.

There's something irresistible about Labrador retriever puppies. Maybe it's the big brown puppy-dog eyes. The wet button noses. The cute floppy ears. The soft downy fur. Or the uncontrollable tail that registers enthusiasm the way a tiny heartbeat flutters excitement.

Of course, it's all of those things—and many others—that we find so appealing in Lab puppies.

T's as if they were born to charm us, beguile us into plucking them from a litter and taking them into our homes.

$\mathcal{W}$e like to think that we've been manipulating dogs for millennia, but the truth is that dogs have been manipulating us for just as long. Who, after all, can refuse a helpless pup?

*E*ven those of us who think there's an element of free will involved have a difficult time in choosing a new Lab puppy.

PUPPIES
4 SALE

The
waterfowler,
for instance,
checks
references,
titles, pedigrees
in his quest to
find a Little
Duck Hunter
that will grow
someday into
a Big Duck
Hunter and
accompany
him afield.

*B*ut when the big day comes and he takes his wife and kids along, he might just as well pick the cute one.

More often than not, the choice has already been made for him.

*M*aybe it's best to leave such decisions in the hands of the young . . . or young at heart.

After all, children and puppies are made for each other. They meet face to face, at a level that is at once below and above that of the adult world.

*M*aybe that's what children and Lab puppies truly have in common. For no matter how old they get, we will always recognize in them an element of eternal youth.

A Day in the Good Life

We should all be so lucky as to be born into this world a Labrador pup. Only Riley had a life this good: free room and board, lots of pampering and pats on the head, no bills to pay, no worries. In fact, aside from being careful about where he relieves himself (and for a time he's even allowed to slide on that), nobody really expects much from the Little Duck Hunter because, well, he's "just a pup."

Life is idyllic (for Pup, at least) those first weeks after you bring him home.

A typical morning begins with a trip outside for a quick constitutional, followed by a cheery calling to the food bowl, which to a pup must be like rising to the smell of fresh coffee percolating, the crackle of ham and eggs sizzling on the stove.

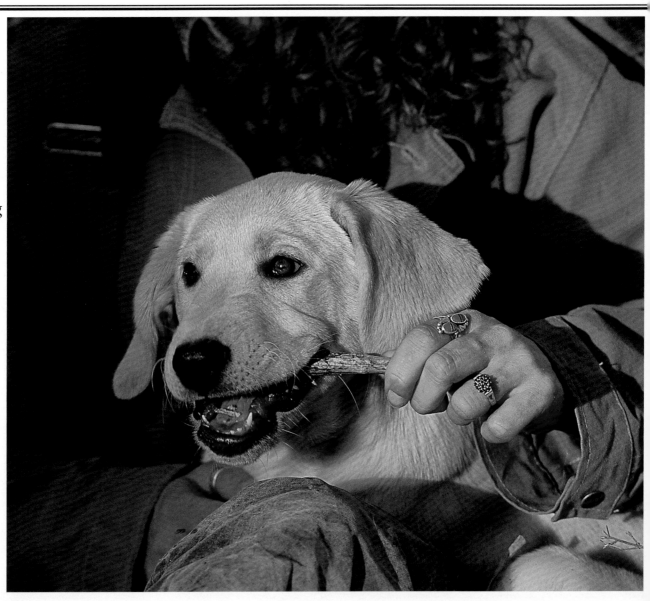

Next order of business: Find something to chew. The Little Duck Hunter makes an art of chewing, putting his toothy signature on everything within reach.

When you consider some of the perks, it doesn't seem so ridiculous coveting the life of a puppy. But the good life is not only a meal ticket and lying around. It's also a lifetime of free healthcare.

Nothing, however, beats a sunny spot on the carpeted floor, except maybe curling up on doggie bed next to the fireplace. Even better is nodding peacefully on the master's lap, dreaming puppy dreams in contented bliss.

All Lab puppies have hunter's blood in their veins. And whether or not they ever become active pursuers of ducks and geese or upland birds, they will always follow their nose, hunting style, and go wherever it leads them.

What we know of the world, we have discovered mostly with our eyes. The Little Duck Hunter, on the other hand, perceives the world in terms of scents and odors. Drive with the car window partially down, and your puppy will strain to stick as much of his nose and head out as possible, taking in the smells of the world as it passes by.

A natural sense of curiosity is the driving force behind all this nosiness. Sometimes this combination of a curious mind and precocious nose can lead to remarkable discoveries, like the alluring scent of the odd-looking creature at the end of your fishing line.

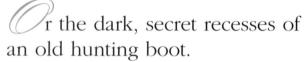

Or the dark, secret recesses of an old hunting boot.

Other times it can lead to trouble, as when the Little Duck Hunter suddenly finds himself on the receiving end of a swat from the family cat. Or when a bag of Puppy Chow is just too tempting to resist.

And occasionally it finds an outlet in just plain innocent fun.

$\mathscr{B}$ut the same nose that proves so good at getting the Little Duck Hunter into things, isn't always as adept at getting him out.

The Little Duck Hunter may have a good sense of smell, but that doesn't mean he likes smelling good. In fact, the opposite is true. If beauty is in the eye of the beholder, then what smells pleasant must be up to the nose of the sniffer. Unfortunately, dead and rotting things, like that pile of old fish heads you buried in the garden, always seem like after-bath body splash to a Lab puppy.

The best advice: Keep plenty of shampoo handy, and don't be afraid of getting a little wet yourself.

At Work and At Play

ll Lab puppies love to play. Like the instinct to retrieve and their innate sense of curiosity, playfulness is something they're born with. Leave them alone with a toy, a sock, or a baseball cap, and they will drag it around, toss it in the air, catch it, run with it. Add another dog or puppy to the mix, and the sport will turn quickly into a game of tug-of-war.

This playfulness is one of the things we find most endearing in Labs. It's why they make great family dogs, and why they get along so famously with children—perhaps the only other creatures who can match their boundless energy and unbridled enthusiasm.

The trick in training the Little Duck Hunter is to blur the edge between work and play until the two become one in the same. For the trainer, it is both a mindset and an exercise in sleight-of-hand. It's thinking of bumpers, whistles, collars, and leads not as *tools* but rather as some of the basic *toys* of the trade.

At work and at play is where you and your charge develop a close-knit bond. You set the game up so that he is sure to succeed. You encourage, praise, and reward him. His confidence in you grows, and so does his confidence in himself.

The Little Duck Hunter can't see the endgame to all this work and play. To him these days are to be cherished for what they are—sheer fun.

And even though you may have your eye on the distant prize, you, too, should relish these special moments . . . for they will not come again.

The Promise of Things To Come

A Lab puppy's first taste of waterfowling may come as part of a game on a sunny hillside with another little duck hunter. In any event, it should come slow and easy.

Though he has the heart and drive of a fully-grown Lab, the Little Duck Hunter is not a Big Duck Hunter yet. These early days are for introductions. Time for him to get his first whiff of real bird scent. To grow accustomed to the sound of a shotgun. To tag along on his first hunting trip.

Boys and adolescent Labs
naturally take to hunting.
It's part of their inheritance.

*F*ollow their footsteps back in time and you're led to the same wild places. Follow their footsteps forward and the circle is complete.

$\mathcal{W}$hat he lacks in size, the Little Duck Hunter more than makes up for in tenacity. His motto seems to be: Where there's a will, there's a way.

Even though deep down he's still an overgrown baby . . .

*B*ut don't worry. There will be time enough tomorrow for the work of Big Duck Hunters.

*N*ow's the time for him to go along for the ride and take it all in.